Marital FITNESS
...2 FIT 2 QUIT

STRENGTH TRAINING FOR MARRIAGE

By Apostle Keith & Pastor Lisa Wesley

Marital Fitness...2 Fit 2 Quit
Strength Training for Marriage

Copyright © 2012 by Apostle Keith & Lisa Wesley

All rights reserved. No portion of this book may be reproduced, stored in a retrieval system, or transmitted in any form or by any means – electronic, mechanical, photocopy, recording, or any other without the prior permission of the author.
ISBN: 978-0-9828379-4-8

Printed in United States of America.

Cover designed by Sharon Dailey

Editing by Brenda Cotton

Inquiries may be addressed to:
newlife@newlifeinchrist.net or
www.keithlisaministries.com

This book is available at special quantity discounts to use as premiums and ministry promotions, or for use in marriage training programs.

To contact a representative please visit www.newlifeinchrist.net or contact the church at 816-966-8989.

DEDICATION

This book is dedicated to our two sons & their wives, Keith, Jr. (Rabihah) and Jabbar (Meka).
We trust God that your marriages will be all that He has purposed in His heart for them to be. You have made our lives full and complete.

We also dedicate this book to all nine of our wonderful grandchildren:

Jordan, Keirra, Kaylah, Jabriyah, Jada, Rhema, Jay, Keyus, and Chase. May these principles be a blessing to you and your future spouses.

CONTENTS

ACKNOWLEDGEMENTS... 9

FOREWORD.. 11

INTRODUCTION... 17

CHAPTER 1.. 24
SPIRITUAL FITNESS *(2 MUCH GOD, 2 LITTLE GOD)*
How to Be Spiritually Balanced

CHAPTER 2.. 43
EMOTIONAL FITNESS *(2 HIGH, 2 LOW)*
Dealing with the High's & Low's of Marriage

CHAPTER 3.. 63
SEXUAL FITNESS *(2 MUCH SEX, 2 LITTLE SEX)*
Sexual Healing for the Bedroom

CHAPTER 4.. 81
FINANCIAL FITNESS *(2 MANY BILLS, 2 LITTLE MONEY)*
Balancing the Checkbook

CHAPTER 5.. 101
PHYSICAL FITNESS *(2 FAT, 2 SKINNY)*
How to Be Physically Fit For the Life of Your Marriage

CHAPTER 6.. 117
FIT FOR ETERNITY

REFERENCES... 122

ACKNOWLEDGEMENTS

First and foremost, we give thanksgiving and praise to our Lord Jesus Christ who not only gave us the opportunity to write this book, but saved us and washed us in His precious blood and wrote our names in the Book of Life. To Him be the glory!

To our wonderful extended family that we owe a wealth of gratitude:
Our parents
Gladys Wesley, who is with the Lord.
Thank you Mom, for your word of prophecy in declaring that our marriage was made in heaven.
&
Marjorie & Earnest Collins
You have exemplified true commitment in Marriage & have always challenged us to excel in the things of God. Thank God, Daddy for your newfound faith in Christ. What a joy divine!

To all of our biological brothers & sisters who have imparted into our lives and supported us in ministry. We love you!

*It is with much love and gratitude that we say thanks
to the New Life in Christ church family,
Thank you for your prayers, encouragement, and
support for 25 years.
May the Lord richly reward you.*

~~~~~~~

*Thank you to Brian & Michelle Gines and
Purpose Publishing. We could not have done this
without you.*

~~~~~~~

*Thank you Tommy & Surrina Greene for believing
in the ministry. You have pushed us to write this
book and now it is done!*

~~~~~~~

*Thank you Brenda Cotton for your gift of editing.
You helped us in the final mile.*

~~~~~~~

*May God bless all of you
& every married couple who will read this book.*

FOREWORD

In this incredible book, **"2 Fit 2 Quit"**, Apostle Keith & Pastor Lisa Wesley have poured out every *"secret"* from God for married couples to live in wedded bliss. In God's Divine order: first comes love, then comes marriage, then comes sex and a baby carriage. [Hebrews 13:4, Ephesians 5:22-33, Colossians 3: 18-19, Jeremiah 28:4-6].

All of us, who personally know the Wesley's, would agree that as a God-fearing couple, they are **"fitly-joined 2gether 4ever"**. Without a doubt, the messages of this book will enhance couples in the way they live and interact *spiritually, emotionally, financially, physically and definitely sexually.*

From cover to cover, in **"2 Fit 2 Quit"** they have captured the very essence of what God intended for marriage. It is a "Divine" institution that came from the Heart of God. Marriage was God's idea; He created the marriage before He ever created the church. God said it was not good for man to be alone, and he created a helpmeet for him, according to Genesis 2:18. God solved the family problem first by creating the union between a man and a woman; man seals the deal with marriage licenses, traditions and ceremonies.

In addition, they so eloquently cover all the areas of the male- female relationship in marriage. We need the fruit of the Spirit [love, joy, peace…] to be manifested in our marriages to deal with our **bad moods** and **negative attitudes**. Consequently, people need *"Marital Fitness"* to enjoy a happy and successful relationship. And truly in all marriages you will find that we need to bring our *"emotion"* under *devotion* to God.

And just when I thought they had said enough, the Wesley's begin to expound upon one of my favorite marital topics: **SEX.** I tell everybody, everywhere, "A **Sexy Spouse** makes a **Happy House**"; "I got a **Good thing** at home, my mind don't need to roam"; "You need a **Song** and a **Thong** to make your marriage **Strong**"; "Every **Good thing** needs a **G-string**."

As I have been ministering all over the world, teaching the revelation of, *Loose the L.O.V.E.--"Loose"* means Loving Our Only Spouse Everyday, and *"LOVE* "means Living Our Vows Everyday. We must learn how to love our spouses for better, or for worse, for richer, or for poorer, in sickness, and in health, until death do us part. Thereby, empowering every marital relationship with the ability to **"4give 2live"**. Couples often find themselves asking the question, *"How do I live with the one I love?"* We have to go to our divine source- -God, who is love. Remember that **Love** and **SEX** are both God's ideas. There are three levels of love: **A**gape (Spiritual love), **P**hileo

(Social love) and **E**ros (Sexual love). So, men, you must go **A.P.E.** over your wife. You must **love** (*Inspire her*), **like** (*Admire her*) and **lust** (*Desire her*).

With an apostolic and pastoral wisdom, the Wesley's give plain and simple advice on the subject of **MONEY**!

I want all you men to know that:

"Romance without Finance ain't got no chance"
"A woman gets mean, when you ain't got no green"
"A woman will act funny, when you ain't got no money"
"Your marriage will crash, if you ain't got no cash"
"Loving gets tight when the money ain't right"

Debt is the leading cause of divorce and destruction in many marital relationships. Thus, couples must learn how to deal wisely with their financial affairs. Ultimately, the book shares how to preserve our physical bodies with healthy nutrition and consistent exercise. We need energy, vitality and strength to finish our course together.

*"Marriage is a **drag**, living with a **nag**, a **hag** and a **bag**; or a **slouch**, a **grouch**, with a **pouch** sleeping on a **couch**.*

> ## A Word of Wisdom for All Husbands:
>
> You must treasure her, you must pleasure her just don't measure her. Never criticize her age, weight, shape or size. Always remember that your **Good Health is your Greatest Wealth!!!**

Apostle Keith & Pastor Lisa, I honor and salute you for writing such an Awesome Book. I strongly encourage and highly recommend that engaged and married couples everywhere read and apply the wisdom of your marital experience.

Exercise your minds, along with your bodies and glean from what they share and your marriages will always be **"2 Fit 2 Quit"**. This book is a must read for marriage preparation and preservation.

We will Submit!
We will Commit!!
We will not Quit!
Our Marriages will be Fit!!!

By His Grace, For His Glory,
Apostle Louis Greenup, Jr.
The Marriage L.O.V.E. Doctor
www.louisgreenup.org

A WORD FROM GOD

Two people are better off than one, for they can help each other succeed. If one person falls, the other can reach out and help. But someone who falls alone is in real trouble. Likewise, two people lying close together can keep each other warm. But how can one be warm alone? A person standing alone can be attacked and defeated, but two can stand back-to-back and conquer. Three are even better, for a triple-braided cord is not easily broken.

Eccl. 4:9-12 (New Living Translation)

INTRODUCTION

The dictionary defines marriage as the social institution under which a man and woman establishes their decision to live as husband and wife by legal commitments, religious ceremonies, etc.

As we approached the writing of this book, we realize that it began as a cry and a burden in our hearts for marriages. It is more than the journalistic effort it takes to finish it. In this present day, the state of marriage as God our Creator designed it, is in jeopardy. The postmodern mindset today is diabolically set to destroy and annihilate this beautiful and holy union that God has created. What God has joined together (holy matrimony between one man and one woman); man is now trying to separate. Many of our children and grandchildren are in danger of losing the joy that comes with this type of union. We must pray, teach, and live out the principles of marriage that God has given us in His Word.

This book is designed for those who want to preserve the sanctity of the marriage union. It is for those who feel they have a healthy marriage, but need a checkup to remain in this condition.

It is for the single man or woman who has a hope and desire to get married, yet fears their dream will not be realized because of the perversions in our world as it relates to marriage. It is also for those who are married and may be contemplating divorce perhaps because of what is called "irreconcilable differences". You may feel you married the wrong person or the two of you don't make a good *'fit'*.

Whatever your position is, we want to encourage you that you can have a good marriage. Just as you can reshape and tone your physical body with exercise, it is possible to recreate and reshape your marriage! We strongly believe that two people can be fitly joined together in marriage -God's style. You don't have to give up on the hope that you and your spouse can stay together "until death do you part". It can happen or else God would not have said it in His Word. All it takes is faith, willpower, effort, and obedience to the Word of God. With the help of the Lord, you too can have a marriage that is **2 Fit 2 Quit.**

Marital Fitness...2 FIT 2 QUIT

STRENGTH TRAINING TIP:

AT THE END OF EACH CHAPTER YOU ARE ENCOURAGED TO CHECK YOUR FITNESS LEVEL. JOURNAL LINES ARE PROVIDED FOR NOTES, IDEAS AND PERSONAL THOUGHTS.

USE THIS AREA TO APPLY WHAT YOU HAVE LEARNED, SO YOUR MARRIAGE WILL BE 2 FIT 2 QUIT.

CHAPTER 1

SPIRITUAL FITNESS: 2 MUCH GOD, 2 LITTLE GOD

How to Be Spiritually Balanced.

They that be whole need not a physician, but they that are sick. *Matt 9:12 KJV*

The following statement is written on all exercise video and DVD material:

> *"Consult with your doctor before beginning this or any exercise routine.*
>
> *The creators, producers, distributors and participants of this program do not assume liability for any injury or loss in connection with this exercise program and instruction therein."*

However, from a biblical perspective, our Creator (God the Father), the Producer (Jesus Christ), the Distributor (The Holy Spirit) will **guarantee** that as you participate in His marital fitness program, and follow the instructions written therein (The Word of God), your marriage will be in good health and prosper, even as your soul prospers (3 John 2) and you will be *2 Fit 2 Quit!*

MEET THE DOCTOR

Let's first review His biography.

He was educated in the school of Eternity.
He is not just a general practitioner, but is an expert in all facets of human care.

He has an extensive list of references. Here are just a few:

- He healed the woman with the issue of blood – Matt. 9:20-22
- He raised Jairus' daughter from the dead – Mark 5:22-23,35-42
- He rebuked the fever of Simon Peter's mother-in-law – Matt. 8:14-15
- He gave sight to Blind Bartimaeus – Mark 10:46-52
- He cast out multiple demons from the man called Legion – Luke 8:30-36
- He rebuked the dumb spirit from a child – Mark 9:16-26
- He cast out 7 devils from Mary Magdalene – Luke 8:2
- He reattached the ear of the servant of the High Priest – Luke 22:49-51
- He died for the sins of all humanity – Isa. 53:4-5

This doctor not only has office hours, but He also makes house calls. Rev. 3:20 says, *"Behold, I stand at the door and knock. If anyone hears My voice and opens the door, I will come in to him and dine with him, and he with Me."* NKJV

We can see that Jesus has every capability and is well qualified to heal, to deliver, and to raise a person from the dead so we know He can restore whatever marital situation you may find yourself in!

With many people, the only time they go to the doctor is when there is an ailment in their body; however, everyone must get an annual checkup, whether healthy or sick. In marriage, we all need to allow the Lord to examine us and if need be, diagnose some things in our life that may not be healthy in our marriage. Every couple at one time or another has marital difficulties, even the healthiest of marriages.

Let's go and see what diagnosis Doctor Jesus has for our marriages.

A Checkup from the Neck Up

The Tongue
There is one who speaks like the piercings of a sword, but the tongue of the wise promotes health. (Prov. 12:18)

Death and life are in the power of the tongue, and those who love it will eat its fruit.
(Prov. 18:21)

I remember a saying from a character in a popular 1970's movie, *"**Uptown Saturday Night**"*. There was a character named Rev. Leroy. One of his most popular messages in the movie was ***"Loose Lips Sink Ships"***. This message rings so true in marriage. How many marriages have been destroyed because of negative and harsh words that have been spoken to each other?

When you go for a doctor's visit, one of the first things that the doctor does is have you stick out your tongue. Sometimes, this is one of the signs of a healthy or unhealthy body.

This is also true in a marital relationship. Words are so powerful. Jesus taught us that words are not just temporal but they are eternal! *Matt 12:36-37,"Let me tell you something: Every one of these careless words is going to come back to haunt you.*

There will be a time of reckoning. Words are powerful; take them seriously. Words can be your salvation. Words can also be your damnation." (The Message Bible)

The old saying, *"Sticks and stones may break my bones, but words will never hurt me"* is definitely untrue. Some of the things we say to each other cut deep and we can never take back our words. They can remain etched in our minds for a lifetime and shape the way we think and how we relate to life. Many of us are still carrying hurts and wounds today because of words that were spoken over us as a child.

God framed the world by His Word (Hebrews 11:3). We also frame our world by our words; likewise, we shape our marriage by speaking the Word of God. After God finished creating both the man and the woman, He declared, *"It is very good" (Gen. 1:31).* Just as God spoke a blessing over His creation, so we must speak blessings over each other. We must first begin to say that our marriage is good. Remember "The Law of First Mention"? It is the first that determines the rest! We must declare that marriage is honorable since it is the first institution that God blessed! So **take divorce out** of your vocabulary. <u>Don't let this bird build a nest in your mind!</u>

Husbands must be like Jesus who washes His bride by His Word!

*Eph 5:25-26...Husbands, love your wives, even as Christ also loved the church, and gave himself for it; That he might sanctify and cleanse it with the washing of water **by the word**, KJV*

*1 Peter 3:10-11..."For let him who wants to enjoy life and see good days [good — whether apparent or not] **keep his tongue free from evil and his lips from guile** (treachery, deceit). Let him turn away from wickedness and shun it, and let him do right. Let him search for peace (harmony; undisturbedness from fears, agitating passions, and moral conflicts) and seek it eagerly. [Do not merely desire peaceful relations with God, with your fellowmen, and with yourself, but pursue, go after them!]"* AMP

This scripture reveals to us that we have a choice of what kind of life we want to live and a great portion of it has to do with the words we speak. Notice how many times the word 'let' is used. This is a strong word because it demonstrates the part we must play. Webster's dictionary defines **let** as *'to free from confinement; to permit to enter, pass, or leave.'* In other words, we can permit or disallow certain things to enter into our lives by what we say. If we want to have a good marriage, we must speak faith into our situation, even if it seems as though it is dead. If we speak doubt and unbelief, it will produce death. We must change our vocabulary and elevate our speech to say what the Word of God says. Until we can speak words that are wholesome to each other, sometimes, the best thing we can do is to say nothing. We need to sit and be quiet and allow the Spirit of God to minister faith into our hearts; otherwise, we can mess up what God wants to do in building up our marriage.

This is what happened to Zacharias. This man of God and his wife were devout and committed to the Lord. They had been praying and believing God for many years for a son, but it seemed to no avail. I can imagine that as the years passed by and Zacharias and Elizabeth were well advanced in age, they probably had become weary and weak in their faith and began to give up hope of having a child. Finally, as he was continuing to serve God in the priesthood, the Lord answered his prayer and sent an angel to tell him that God had heard his prayer. He and Elizabeth would soon have a son. Zacharias was so unsure that he began to question the angel of the Lord and asked, *"How can I be sure this will happen? I'm an old man now, and my wife is also well along in years."* The Lord shut his mouth so that the blessing that he had been praying for so many years would not be hindered by his unbelief (Luke 1:18-20).

Many times, we pray and ask God to change things, but we can make our prayers null and void by speaking just the opposite of what we asked God to do. We can't give up on God. He can bring life to anything, including a dead, dried up marriage.

It is so vitally important that we speak the right words; first of all to ourselves, and then to each other. Learning this one principle alone would cause less divorces and domestic violence in our homes. *"Pleasant words are like a honeycomb, Sweetness to the soul and health to the bones."* (Prov. 16:24)

They say that you can catch more flies with honey than you can with vinegar. During a heated conflict (which all marriages have), think about what you are going to say before you speak. Stop for a moment and ask yourself this question, *"How would I react if these same words that I am about to say to my spouse were being spoken to me?"* We recognize that sometimes, we must speak truth. No relationship can be built or endure on lies. However, even if it is the truth, it can be spoken in love (Eph. 4:15). Our whole goal and desire should be to edify and build up each other, not tear down.

> **"You can catch more flies with honey than you can with vinegar".**

In the book of Job there is a powerful truth that deals with words. Job 6:25a says *"How forcible are right words!"* Another translation says, *"How pleasing are upright words" (Bible in Basic English)!* Our words are a powerful force in the universe. They are one of the strongest vehicles we have to communicate our thoughts and feelings. We must choose them wisely and carefully.

What kind of marriage do you want? Say what you want and not what you have. It requires tremendous training and discipline to control the tongue. This training must be exercised by both the husband and the wife. Why? Women have a tendency to be more vocal and fight with words. Men tend to be more physical and in general are able to control their tongue.

Yet there are times when men need to speak up and say what they desire. Sometimes, it's not what you say that can hurt you, but it's also what you don't say. You have not because you ask not (James 4:2b). Communication is two-way. God did not make any of us to be mind readers. He designed us to have a mouth to speak and ears to hear. We must use both in order to communicate what is in our heart.

There is a prayer that I pray all the time found in Psalms 141:3. *"Set a watch, O Lord, before my mouth; keep the door of my lips."* I can't say that I have mastered this, but it really helps when I feel I have the need to give my husband a "piece of my mind." I have to call on the Lord to help me speak the mind of Christ. Instead of giving him a piece of my mind, I need to give him a "piece of peace", which comes from the Prince of Peace.

> **Instead of giving your spouse a peace of your mind, give them a "piece of peace."**

The tongue can only be tamed by the Holy Spirit. That's why on the day of Pentecost in Acts 2, the first anatomy of the body that He touched was the tongue. James 3:8 says that it is an unruly evil and can be tamed by no man. We need to call on Dr. Jesus to send us aid. And He has sent the paraclete, the Holy Spirit to assist us. Let's cooperate with Him so that we can have a healthy marriage because we speak the right things.

The Ear

The ear tests the words it hears just as the mouth distinguishes between foods. Job 12:11 NLT

When both of our sons were young, sometimes they would come down with a fever. We would take them to the doctor and one of the things he did would be to check their ears. It was amazing that the majority of the time, his diagnosis would be an ear infection. We thought that was strange and began to doubt his judgment. Later, we found out that research has shown that 90% of the illnesses with infants and children stem from ear infections.

A lot of time, our marriages are infected by listening to wrong counsel. You see, our ears are like a gate, or an entry point of influence. We must be careful what we open them up to hear. Think about the influence that your hearing has in your life. It can be a blessing or it can be devastating!

This started at the beginning. Eve allowed her ear-gate to be opened up to the wrong thing. She listened to the devil say, *"Hath God said?"* She received ungodly counsel against what God had told her. This introduced confusion into the first marriage and caused it to be passed down to this present day.

We are instructed in the Word of God to be careful of listening to bad counsel. Ps 1:1a says, *"Blessed is the man who walks not in the counsel of the ungodly."* Unfortunately, the culture of our day has perverted God's original design for marriage.

As Christians, we must be careful that we don't get ensnared by listening to their counsel. It doesn't matter if the laws are being changed, we must stay with the Biblical pattern and stand in the counsel of the LORD.

Jeremiah 23:18...For who hath stood in the counsel of the Lord, and hath perceived and heard his word? who hath marked his word, and heard it?

Psalm 33:11...The counsel of the Lord stands forever, the thoughts of his heart to all generations.

It is equally important that we take heed to how we hear each other. Many times, there are unresolved conflicts in a marriage because both parties are screaming so loud, that neither of them is listening. If they would only quiet down, and listen to not only what is being said with the mouth, but what the heart is saying, they would come to an understanding. We must train our ears to discern the heart of our mate.

Song of Solomon 8:13...O you who dwell in the gardens, your companions have been listening to your voice — now cause me to hear it. AMP

The challenge in communicating and resolving conflict is making the other person hear what is being said from the heart.

> "I have made a covenant with my eyes; Why then should I look upon another?"

The Eyes

Luke 11:34-36...*Your eye is the lamp of your body. When your eye is healthy, your whole body is full of light. But when your eye is bad, your whole body is full of darkness. Therefore, see to it that the light in you isn't darkness.* (Common English Bible)

CAUTION: OBJECTS IN MIRROR ARE CLOSER THAN THEY APPEAR

Over the years, the automobile industry has improved upon the safety of our cars tremendously. The above statement is a safety warning that is required on all vehicles and is to be engraved on the passenger's side of the rearview mirror. This warning serves to remind the driver not to make a sudden maneuver or change lanes because he/she may **_assume_** that another vehicle is traveling at a safe distance behind him. The object in the mirror is closer than it appears; therefore one must exercise caution.

This speaks volumes to marriage. There must be a warning sign imprinted upon the heart of both a husband and wife to stay in the right lane.

The right lane is the lane where your spouse is. One of the things that have kept us together for forty years is that both of us have not only made a covenant with one another, but a covenant with our eyes that we will only have eyes for each other (Job 31:1). This is not to say that neither of us has ever been tempted, but our love and commitment that we made to God and one another is stronger than our desire to have a few moments of passionate pleasure with someone else.

Sometimes, we can allow a person other than our spouse to get too close to us. It may start out small and innocent but before long, we get involved in a relationship that leads to an adulterous affair.

The first look may be only flirting, but flirting can lead to other things that- sometimes can take you into dangerous territory. There was a song out many years ago that said, *"Just one look, that's all it took."* But the second look can be deadly. Even our Lord knew this as we see in the account of the woman caught in adultery (John 8:3). Jesus took one look at the woman, who was obviously brought to him barely clothed, but He kept looking down to the ground. He knew not to look up again. Remember, Jesus was not only God, but He was fashioned as a man.

He was tempted in all points as we are, yet He did not sin. In His humanity, He demonstrated to all of us how to overcome temptations.

Now Isaac came from the way of Beer Lahai Roi, for he dwelt in the South. And Isaac went out to meditate in the field in the evening; and he lifted his eyes and looked, and there, the camels were coming. Then Rebekah lifted her eyes, and when she saw Isaac she dismounted from her camel; 62 for she had said to the servant, "Who is this man walking in the field to meet us?" The servant said, "It is my master." So she took a veil and covered herself. And the servant told Isaac all the things that he had done. Then Isaac brought her into his mother Sarah's tent; and he took Rebekah and she became his wife, and he loved her. So Isaac was comforted after his mother's death. Gen 24:62-67 NKJV

Isaac and Rebekah both demonstrate to us what it means to have a single eye as it relates to marriage. It was "love at first sight". Isaac had eyes only for Rebekah. The moment she mounted off the camel, he took her as his wife. We never see in scripture where he was interested in another woman. This resulted in a lifetime commitment to one another. Unlike his father Abraham, who had perpetual infighting and conflict in his family because of his many wives, Isaac and Rebekah had no domestic drama around their marriage!

This story reminds me of the first time I saw Lisa. She was the new girl that came to my high school and this was, if you will, my 'Rebekah moment'. I was a senior and she was a junior. I was so mesmerized that I had to meet her! A friend of mine went to the same church as her, and he introduced me to the woman who would become my wife for life. In fact, I asked her to marry me two weeks after I met her. She said no at first, but two years later we got married. Hallelujah!

The eye-gate relates to both husband and wife. However, men must be very cautious in this area because they are motivated by what they see, whereas women are turned on by what they hear. There is an epidemic of pornography in the United States that is predominant with men. Statistics shows that 72% of men and only 28% of women are caught up in this deadly trap.

> **The movies are <u>moving</u> many to sin.**

We must be cautious about what we allow to enter into our eye-gate by even being selective of what we watch on television and the movies. The media is one of the key instruments the devil uses to bring destruction and perversion into our home. Television is doing just what it says, "telling a vision". The movies are moving many to sin. There is H.B.O. (Hell Bound Only); Cinemax (which makes you sin to the max); and Showtime (which leaves you no time for God). Much of what we see is not the vision that God has designed for marriage.

The Heart

...Jesus said to him, "'You shall love the LORD your God with all your heart, with all your soul, and with all your mind. This is the first and great commandment. And the second is like it: 'You shall love your neighbor as yourself.' Matt 22:37-39 NKJV

As we conclude our examination, we cannot forget to check the heart. This is one of the major organs of the body. When the heart stops beating, life ends.

A good marriage will last for a lifetime when both hearts are beating strong for the Lord. Since God is the one who designed marriage, it stands to reason that He knows what it takes to keep a marriage healthy and strong. We must have an ongoing, vital relationship with Him first of all.

It is so important that Christian couples worship the same God, and as much as possible, in the same house of worship. Both couples need to be hearing and taught the Word of God together.

"Can two walk together except they be agreed?" (Amos 3:3) There is a spiritual intimacy that takes place when we enter into worship together. We can see this taking place in the corporate gathering. Have you ever noticed the bond that develops between the members of a local church? When we come together and worship the one true God in Spirit and in truth, an affinity takes place. That is why the corporate gathering is so important. We need fellowship with God and with His people. How much more is this spiritual bonding needed in a marriage relationship?

Yet, there may be times when there is an irregular heartbeat that takes place in a marriage, meaning that one person is pursuing God and the other isn't, or one spouse is an unbeliever. The Bible calls this being *"unequally yoked." (See 2 Cor. 6:14)*

When my husband and I first got married, he was not saved and wasn't thinking about the Lord. I was raised in church so I knew God, to a measure. We did not get any premarital counseling because that was not one of the teachings of the denomination of my church. However, from the time I was a child, it was always in my heart to marry a man who would love me, and when I met Keith, he fit this portion of the bill, (or so I thought).

So we got married and went to college together. I would pray every night that God would save him. Boy, did God answer that prayer! At first, it was too much for me. I wanted God to save him, but not so radically! But God does all things well! He had a plan that superseded mine. Forty years later, with two children, and nine grandchildren, God's plan has continued to unfold in our lives. This is the Lord's work and it is marvelous in our eyes.

I say this to encourage those of you who may have a spouse that is not walking with the Lord. Don't give up! Keep praying and believing God who is able to do exceeding abundantly above all that we can ask or think according to the power that is at work in you (Eph. 3:20). God has given us a promise in His Word.

1 Cor. 7:14-16...For the Christian wife brings holiness to her marriage, and the Christian husband brings holiness to his marriage. Otherwise, your children would not be holy, but now they are holy. Don't you wives realize that your husbands might be saved because of you? And don't you husbands realize that your wives might be saved because of you? (New Living Translation)

So, let me ask you, how fit is your marriage spiritually? Can you really have too much God, or is there too little of God in your marriage?

If you are reading this book, and have never received Jesus Christ as your Lord and Savior, we urge you to do so today. Chapter 6 will give you instructions on how to be saved. This is the first foundational step in order to have a marriage that is 2 FIT 2 QUIT.

1

MY SPIRITUAL FITNESS, AM I SPIRITUALLY FIT?

_____
_____
_____
_____
_____
_____
_____
_____
_____
_____
_____
_____
_____
_____
_____

POWER LIFT:
The tongue, eyes, ears and heart require continual checking up. The Lord is the cure for all.

CHAPTER 2

**EMOTIONAL FITNESS: 2 HIGH, 2 LOW
WHAT'S THE HAPPY MEDIUM?**

Dealing with the High's & Low's of Marriage

"I'm not leaving, I'm cleaving" is a statement every married couple should make. However, when we make this statement, our emotions should not be the driving force in keeping the commitment. When our emotions control us, we begin to make decisions based on whatever feelings we have at that moment. It has been said that feelings make good slaves, but poor masters!

The right attitude can transform the atmosphere of our marriage, but negative emotions can sometimes be the leak that brings in a flood of troubles. Unchecked emotions can deceive you. People who are slaves to their emotions don't have a reality of who they are. There is a disconnection with who they are and how they feel. How you feel does not dictate who you are. Some days, I don't feel like being married, but that doesn't change the truth that I am a wife. Some days I don't feel like I'm anointed, but the anointed one lives and abides in me, for the anointing is Christ in me, the hope of glory (Col. 1:27).

We must get our emotions in check. We must learn to rule our emotions and not let our emotions rule us. Emotions are good, because God gave them to us when He created us. But we can choose to let them lead us to good or to bad. Many times, we don't realize we are being led by our feelings and not the Spirit of God, nor obedience to His Word. We can have distorted affections and diluted passions. More and more people are having emotional issues, especially as it relates to marriage.

Being led by our emotions can cause us to be irrational and make wrong decisions such as divorce or get involved in an extramarital affair. Sometimes after a couple has been married for a long period of time, they **"feel"** the thrill is gone. Many make the statement, *"I fell out of love with him or her."* Their answer is divorce. You don't have to act out your feelings. You act on the fact and the feeling will follow the act! We must act on the truth of God's Word concerning marriage. That is what we must be committed to.

> **"Feelings make good slaves, but poor masters!"**

Matt 19:5-8...'For this reason a man shall leave his father and mother and be joined to his wife, and the two shall become one flesh'? So then, they are no longer two but one flesh. Therefore what God has joined together, let not man separate." They said to Him, "Why then did Moses command to give a certificate of divorce, and to put her away?" He said to them, "Moses, because of the hardness of your hearts, permitted you to divorce your wives, but from the beginning it was not so. NKJV

In this scripture, Jesus is making a strong statement concerning divorce. When a person's heart is hardened, it is because they have allowed their emotions to become unsanctified and unyielded to God's grace to keep them together.

Negative emotions are the residue from the old man. Our emotions need to go through a 'catharsis,' a purification or purging that brings about spiritual renewal or release from tension. So what is the remedy? The Word of God is a catharsis for our emotions. It is His Word that gives us the **power** to cleave, and never leave.

Heb 4:12-13...For the word of God is alive and powerful. It is sharper than the sharpest two-edged sword, cutting between soul and spirit, between joint and marrow. It exposes our innermost thoughts and desires. (NLT)

innermost thoughts and desires. (NLT)

We have experienced the power of God's Word at work in our own lives. One of the reasons that we have been able to stay together for almost forty years is because we have made it our intention to submit ourselves and apply the principles of the scriptures and allow them to daily renew our minds. It is a choice that we have made. We choose to obey God, and not our emotions.

As we said, our emotions can take us on a wild roller-coaster ride and cause us to do irrational things. But the Word of God gives sound judgment when we face difficult situations.

There are times when one of us has wanted to have our own way and do our own thing; in spite of the other. But usually, one or the other will yield and submit to the will of God through His Word. We won't tell you that we have always yielded peacefully nor immediately. Our individual wants and desires are very strong. It is not easy to give up when you believe that you are right. But there comes a place and time when we must ask ourselves, *"Do we want **what** is right or do we want to **be** right?"* This is called a denial of self or the cross. When this takes place, the peace of God rules our hearts and there is harmony between us once again.

I'm finding more and more that Christians are having so many emotional issues because we simply don't study the Word of God nor apply the principles enough to renew our minds. We become a victim to our own thoughts, and slaves to the dictates of our feelings, which are influenced by this worldly system. Many have been wounded and hurt in the past and still carry these hurts today; thus their whole life is run by a gamut of negative emotions.

The Bible says, *"If any man be in Christ, he is a new creature" (2 Cor. 5:17).* Jesus can heal damaged emotions. Christ nailed them to the cross. We must recognize ourselves to be dead to these negative emotions.

Isa 53:5...But he was wounded for our transgressions, he was bruised for our iniquities: the chastisement of our peace was upon him; and with his stripes we are healed. (KJV)

Jesus was wounded for our transgressions so we could be emotionally healed. The crown of thorns placed upon his head was for the healing of our mind and emotions. He was hung up for our hang-ups. Our responsibility is to crucify the flesh and release our emotions to the Lord.

Gal 5:24-26...Those who belong to Christ Jesus have nailed the passions and desires of their sinful nature to his cross and crucified them there. Since we are living by the Spirit, let us follow the spirit's leading **in every part of our lives**. Let us not become conceited, or provoke one another, or be jealous of one another. (NLT)

In other words, don't let your emotions wreck your future by their ups and downs. Gal. 5:26 tells that unchecked or uncrucified emotions makes us conceited, argumentative, and jealous!

"Jesus was hung up for our hang ups."

It takes two whole people to make a lasting marriage. Many times, we go into marriage with the concept that each of us makes up one half of the marriage and when the two halves come together, the marriage is whole. But with God, 1 (God) +1 (whole husband) +1 (whole wife) =1 blessed marital union. This depicts the trinity of marriage. Both parties need to be pursuing a vibrant, living relationship with Jesus Christ in order for the marriage to be one whole union.

Don't let your emotions cloud sound judgment. Apostle Skip Horton

Every marriage will go through high and low periods. However, in order to sustain the marriage and live out the vows we made to God and each other, we must get our emotions under control and maintain balance.

When our emotions and feelings are left unchecked, chaos, disorder, and confusion are the result. Eve listened to the devil and got caught up in her emotions. He deceived her by planting a lie that God was holding out on her. He planted the thought in her mind that she was made as an inferior creature. He blinded her to the fact that she was already like God because she (just like her husband, Adam) was created in His image!

Gen 3:4-5..."You won't die!" the serpent replied to the woman. "God knows that your eyes will be opened as soon as you eat it, and you will be like God, knowing both good and evil." (New Living Translation)

As a result, their marriage became dysfunctional. They lost the genuine intimacy they had with God and each other. They lost their home and we see chaos and violence entering into the family. This dysfunction in the family has been passed down to every generation, even to this day. We must break this generational curse, or should we say, "generational chaos".

The bad news is, it's not our house anymore.

BREAKING THE ADDICTION TO CHAOS

Our world, and in particular marriage, is becoming more and more chaotic, or should we say, **'out of order'**.

In an interview with young adults, George Barna said, *"Today's generation wants their marriage to last, but are not particularly optimistic about that possibility. There is also evidence that many young people are moving toward embracing the idea of **'serial marriage'**, in which a person gets married two or three times, seeking a different partner for each phase of their adult life."*

In Matt. 19:8, Jesus was addressing the chaos and disorder that man has brought to himself and the world because of the iniquity of our hearts. *"Moses, because of the hardness of your hearts, permitted you to divorce your wives, but from the beginning it was not so".* He points them back to the beginning, the genesis of marriage, when God had established order to the cosmos, which was full of darkness. Once Adam and Eve (the first married couple) sinned, it threw the whole world into a perpetual cycle of chaos and disorder, especially in marriage.

Divorce is one of the things that can throw a family into chaos. It can be very traumatic to a husband and wife, and even moreso to a child. No one wins in a divorce. Jesus was not utterly condemning divorce because He gives one stipulation for divorce, which is when one person violates the marriage covenant through adultery.

Matt. 19:9a, *"And I say unto you, Whosoever shall put away his wife, except it be for fornication, and shall marry another, committeth adultery..."* He was addressing the root cause, man's rebellion against the will of God as it relates to marriage, which results in a hardening of one's heart.

We see an alarming divorce rate not only in our society, but in the church as well that has become addictive.

There are addictive behaviors of various kinds such as drugs, sex, food, and gambling, just to name a few. However, there are two addictions that are stronger than these and both are detrimental to a marriage relationship. What are they?

1. Addiction to chaos
2. Addiction to quitting (giving up)

These two addictions go hand in hand. We recognize that conflict and trials come to all of us and each of us handles the stress that arises through them differently. But for some, when there is too much chaos, their emotions get the best of them or the pain becomes so unbearable that they begin to look for outside substances to help them cope with the stress. The more they begin to partake of them, the more addictive they become. Sooner or later, their life begins to spiral down and they demonstrate a pattern of abnormal and confusing behavior.

Likewise, with others, they may throw their hands up in despair and say, *"I'm out of here. I can't take it anymore!"* This progresses into an addictive behavior because this becomes the way in which they deal with every problem. They develop a spirit of divorce.

When things go bad, they quit their jobs, leave their church, divorce their spouse, and forsake their children. These addictive behaviors throw the household and family into confusion and chaos. The dictionary says chaos is *"a state of utter confusion or disorder; a total lack of organization; a disruption in the normal order of things."*

Addiction is defined as *"a primary chronic disease of the brain's created functions of reward, motivation, and memory."* God has created us with a brain that is pre-wired to have three circuits: a reward circuit; a memory circuit; and a motivational circuit. Once we are addicted to substances or behaviors that are detrimental, these circuit systems can break down or become distorted. When a person is addicted to chaos, unknowingly they enjoy being rewarded by pain, confusion (mess), and drama. In this condition, what is abnormal seems normal to them. They love darkness more than light. We can see this illustrated today in the *"reality"* television shows. Jesus himself explained it in John 3:19-21...

"And this is the condemnation, that the light has come into the world, and men loved darkness rather than light, because their deeds were evil. For everyone practicing evil hates the light and does not come to the light, lest his deeds should be exposed. But he who does the truth comes to the light, that his deeds may be clearly seen, that they have been done in God." NKJV

This person eventually gets married and the marriage doesn't last because they have damaged emotions and a distorted view of things. They can't understand God's way of blessing two people in marriage; thus, chaos ensues. Many times, it is displayed by abusive behavior. We can see this exemplified in the popular movie, *"The Color Purple"*. The father had a mindset that disrespected and abused women. His son depicted this same abusive behavior with his wife, Celie.

This is why our mind must be renewed and our thoughts reshaped concerning marriage. A mind that is not renewed doesn't **think** they can be happy. There is no faith operating to believe they can love each other for life and cleave and never leave. That is why the brain must be **_reset_** to think differently in terms of reward, motivation, and memory.

Rom 12:1-2...I beseech you therefore, brethren, by the mercies of God, that you present your bodies a living sacrifice, holy, acceptable to God, which is your reasonable service. And do not be conformed to this world, but be transformed by the renewing of your mind, that you may prove what is that good and acceptable and perfect will of God. NKJV

Our minds must go through a process of being renewed and our circuit system must be reset so we can appreciate God's plan to bless us. This takes place once we are saved and regenerated.

Then we begin to understand that God wants to reward us with a good life. It's called the transformation of the total man. You see God is committed to and intent upon changing your and I in our spirit, soul, and body. God is interested in the whole man.

1 Thess 5:23 says, Now may the God of peace Himself sanctify you completely; and may your whole spirit, soul, and body be preserved blameless at the coming of our Lord Jesus Christ. (NKJV)

This is why the cross is so important in our lives. The cross brings deliverance and freedom from the chains of sin. Jesus was crucified on the cross of Calvary so that sin no longer has power over us. We can have the abundant life (John 10:10). And He encourages every believer to take up that cross and follow Him.

Matt 16:24-25... Then Jesus said to his disciples, "If any of you wants to be my follower, you must turn from your selfish ways, take up your cross, and follow me. If you try to hang on to your life, you will lose it. But if you give up your life for my sake, you will save it. New Living Translation

These are strong words given from our Lord, but the cross is essential to every believer's walk of victory. It is even more crucial in marriage.

Marriage in its true sense will teach you how to deny yourself because it is the blending of two lives together and the crossing out of the individual life. Every problem, attitude, or disagreement in marriage requires a cross application. If ever there was an illustration of how the cross works in our lives, it is in the marriage union.

Let's take a look at the cross in these three aspects as it relates to marriage.

The first area is what is called a **cross-out**. This is the dying of the old man and removal of self-centeredness. In marriage, you no longer live the single life. Decisions should be made with your spouse in mind and what will be good for the two of you. We always say whenever someone is added to your life, it requires a new dying. When you add a wife or husband, you as an individual are crossed out. Your life is not your own, but now is blended into one. When you add a child, both husband and wife are crossed out and the child's welfare should take pre-eminence. With the birthing of each child, a little more of you gets crossed out. This is what is required if you want to be a good parent.

The second area is the **cross-point**. This is the point where your passions are confronted by the will of your mate. For example, typically men have stronger sex drives than women.

These drives are heightened during times of stress because in general, men relieve their stress through sexual activity; whereas for some women, sex is the last thing on her mind. She may get relief through her tears, exercise, or just being left alone. When it comes to having an intimate time with each other, the woman may complain of a headache or flatly say to her husband that she doesn't feel like having sex. The man may get upset and feel rejected by his wife.

But when the cross is working, one or the other spouse will yield. The husband will consider his wife's stress level and deny himself. He may run her bath water, make her some tea, or do something that will calm her down. Likewise, the wife will consider that her husband has had a stressful day and submit to his desire. In our own marriage, many times we have found out that once we submit to the will of the other, we feel better and there is greater non-sexual as well as physical intimacy later.

And for a marriage to be sound, you cannot continue to deny one another in the area of sex for long periods of time. Many marriages run into problems of infidelity because they do not address this issue openly. We will discuss more on the sexual relationship in Chapter 3.

> **A little Humor from Apostle Louis Greenup**
> One brother said I am married to a nun. "I don't get **'none'** on Sunday, **'none'** on Monday, and **'none'** on Tuesday, Wednesday, Thursday, Friday, and Saturday.

The third area is the cross-movement. This is the place of Godly satisfaction where you completely yield yourself to the will of God as it relates to marriage. When you get to this place, marriage becomes an enjoyable experience, rather than an endurance contest. You have progressively moved from being independent of your spouse to a place of interdependence upon each other.

As married couples, we must learn how to focus on the main point, which is marital harmony, rather than the momentary displeasure and inconvenience. Dealing with these three aspects of the cross in marriage will stimulate a healthy emotional relationship and cause you to become *2 Fit 2 Quit!*

EXERCISE TIME

As a couple, make this declaration,

"I'm not leaving, I'm cleaving. We stand together in faith to break all addictions to chaos in our marriage. We stand together in faith to break all addictions to quitting. Divorce is not in our vocabulary." **I declare, I'm not leaving! I'm cleaving! In Jesus Name! Amen**

1 Corinthians 13:4-8 reveals the true definition of what real love is.

4 Love endures long and is patient and kind; love never is envious nor boils over with jealousy, is not boastful or vainglorious, does not display itself haughtily. 5 It is not conceited (arrogant and inflated with pride); it is not rude (unmannerly) and does not act unbecomingly. Love (God's love in us) does not insist on its own rights or its own way, for it is not self-seeking; it is not touchy or fretful or resentful; it takes no account of the evil done to it [it pays no attention to a suffered wrong].

6 It does not rejoice at injustice and unrighteousness, but rejoices when right and truth prevail. 7 Love bears up under anything and everything that comes, is ever ready to believe the best of every person, its hopes are fadeless under all circumstances, and it endures everything [without weakening]. 8 Love never fails [never fades out or becomes obsolete or comes to an end]. AMP

Examine the following statements and you and your spouse make the necessary changes in your life in order to bring about **Marital Fitness.**

- ♥ Cleaving couples change their vocabulary from 'I' and 'mine', to 'yours' and 'ours'.

- ♥ Cleaving couples don't have separate accounts that the other is not included on.

- ♥ Cleaving couples do things together (i.e. dates, recreation, shopping, vacations).

- ♥ Cleaving couples raise their children in unity under the guidance of the Lordship of Jesus Christ and His Holy Word.

- ♥ Cleaving couples suffer one for another in times of transition (in sickness and in health, for richer or for poorer, for better or for worse).

Marital Fitness...2 FIT 2 QUIT

2

MY EMOTIONAL FITNESS, ARE MY EMOTIONS IN GOOD SHAPE?

_____
_____
_____
_____
_____
_____
_____
_____
_____
_____
_____
_____
_____

POWER LIFT:
The emotional well-being of each spouse is required for optimal marital fitness.

CHAPTER 3

SEXUAL FITNESS: 2 MUCH SEX, 2 LITTLE SEX

Sexual Healing for the Bedroom

God created man for his pleasure. *Rev 4:11 .... Thou art worthy, O Lord, to receive glory and honour and power: for thou hast created all things, and for thy pleasure they are and were created. KJV*

He put him in a place of pleasure called Eden, which means 'delight'. *Gen 2:15...And the Lord God took the man, and put him into the Garden of Eden to dress it and to keep it.*

He made him a woman to bring him pleasure. *Gen 2:21-23...And the Lord God caused a deep sleep to fall upon Adam and he slept: and he took one of his ribs, and closed up the flesh instead thereof; And the rib, which the Lord God had taken from man, made he a woman, and brought her unto the man. And Adam said, This is now bone of my bones, and flesh of my flesh: she shall be called Woman, because she was taken out of Man. (KJV)*

He gave them a relationship of pleasure – marriage. *Gen 2:24-25...Therefore shall a man leave his father and his mother, and shall cleave unto his wife: and they shall be one flesh. And they were both naked, the man and his wife, and were not ashamed.*

We must see our spouse as a pleasure and not a problem. Eve was created as a solution to a problem. The man Adam was lonely, even though he had a relationship with the Lord. God saw that He needed someone with whom he could be intimate with.

- Your wife is a trophy of grace, not a trophy of troubles
- Your husband is a pillar of power, not a pillar of problems
- Wives are to be helpmates, not hell-mates
- Husbands are the head, not the tail

Our Creator designed marriage to be a pleasurable experience. The sexual union between a husband and a wife is to be enjoyed by both of them.

Prov. 5:15-19...Drink water from your own well—share your love only with your wife. Why spill the water of your springs in the streets, having sex with just anyone? You should reserve it for yourselves. Never share it with strangers. Let your wife be a fountain of blessing for you. Rejoice in the wife of your youth. She is a loving deer, a graceful doe.

Let her breasts satisfy you always. May you always be captivated by her love. (NLT).

When sex is introduced into a person's life in the wrong way, or when a person has been sexually violated, they may develop an unhealthy view of sex because the conscience becomes defiled. Premarital sex can also be damaging to sexual intimacy between married couples. This is true in both men and women. There needs to be a healing that takes place in their heart and a renewing in their minds. This is possible once there is repentance from sin and forgiveness. The blood of Jesus will deliver you from the guilt of sin.

1 John 1:9...If we confess our sins, He is faithful and just to forgive us our sins and to cleanse us from all unrighteousness. (NKJV)

Many couples don't enjoy the beauty of sexual intimacy because they have never taken this step to being healed. Because they have been introduced to sex in an inappropriate manner, the act of sexual intercourse is deemed dirty. But our Creator never designed anything that was not good for us and sexual intercourse between a husband and wife is meant to be enjoyed.

Intercourse is not limited to sex only. There are six types of intercourse:

    Spiritual   Emotional
    Mental/intellectual Social
    Verbal   Physical/sexual

In order to have a healthy marriage, a husband and wife needs to be able to engage in all of these areas, not just the physical or sexual. Why? There may come a time when one spouse cannot participate sexually due to medical reasons. You can't base your whole marriage on one moment of sexual pleasure. The true "climax" comes when the two have engaged in all areas of intercourse.

Intercourse means *"to have dealings or communication between individuals"*. *"It is an interchange of thoughts and feelings"*. In other words, it is a form of communication and a way of interacting between two people. In order to have marital fitness, we should be able to communicate and stimulate one another on all of the above levels.

In the previous chapters, we addressed the importance of being spiritually and emotionally fit, which includes dealing with our verbal and mental intercourse with each other. Before we talk about sexual intimacy, we want to take a moment to address the need for social intercourse.

Marriage starts with two people becoming both lover and friend. Make your spouse your best friend, not just your business or ministry partner.

*Song 5:16...His mouth is most sweet, Yes, he is altogether lovely. This is my beloved, **and this is my friend,** O daughters of Jerusalem! (NKJV)*

Learn to genuinely like your spouse without trying to change them; appreciate the differences you have. It took a while, but we had to learn how to appreciate each other's different personalities and allow those differences to complement not compete with each other. It takes a positive and a negative in order to produce power. Once a couple learns how God has wired each of them, together they can be a powerful force to break the generational strongholds that are plaguing families.

Friendship centers on a mutual experience with each other. What are the activities you both enjoy? When we were first married, we spent a lot of time together. At one time, we even worked at the same company, and we have always worshipped together in the same church. Today, we even like going shopping together, although this was a huge transition for my husband, Keith. I have to confess that there is one area in which I have not gained the victory and that's watching a game with him. I have never been thrilled about sports. I need the work of the cross to be applied in this area.

Sometimes people would ask us, *"Don't you get tired of being around each other so much?"* Some of my husband's friends would joke with him and call him "henpecked." But he always says, *"I'm pecked by the right hen."* I have my own personal saying about spending time with my husband. *"He is like American Express to me. I don't leave home without him."* Don't let the views of others rob you of quality time together.

A husband and wife should be each other's best friend. Many people may not understand having this type of intimacy, but it is vital in a marriage. God has uniquely fitted and joined the two of you in every way. This is not to say that we shouldn't have friends, but there should be no one else who can share the place of social intimacy like your spouse. We must not allow others to violate that space which is reserved only for one another.

A wife's best friend should definitely not be someone of the opposite sex, nor should a husband's best friend be someone of the opposite sex. This can be deadly and dangerous. Be careful of sharing all your intimate and personal issues with others.

One of the things we believe all couples must learn is how to deal with the folk factor: kin folk; church folk; and competing folk. If not kept in their proper place, people can bring separation and destruction to a marriage. You must guard this intimacy and not let anyone else get in that space. When there is a violation, just like Adam and Eve, you have allowed an intruder into your relationship. At this point, trust must be rebuilt.

Conflict always arises in any relationship. Genuine friendship develops when both choose to listen to each other with concern, honesty, and concentration. Make a conscious effort to act in love and let the peace of God rule in your heart. Peace is not the absence of action; it is the absence of reaction. You don't have to react in anger, but sometimes during a heated argument, the best action you can take is to be quiet and pray.

Sexual Intimacy

The sexual union between a man and a woman is very important. It is the consummation of the marriage union. It is an expression of love; thus we call it 'lovemaking'. When engaged in the right way, it can be a beautiful expression of devoted love between husband and wife.

Before there is intercourse, there must be romance. Romance doesn't begin in the bedroom; it starts at the moment the two of you awaken to each other. After the Lord created Eve, he awakened Adam from his deep sleep and brought her to him. When Adam opened his eyes and saw her, he took her unto himself and then declared, *"This is now bone of my bone and flesh of my flesh."* (Gen. 2:23) Adam discovered his wife and was awakened to all the wonder and beauty of this created being that God made for him alone. It is not in scripture, but in my sanctified imagination, I believe they had an intimate moment with each other.

There must be an awakening of our consciousness of each other. Many couples take one another for granted and have never taken a good look to appreciate what they have. So the romance dies and as B. B. King says, *"The thrill is gone!"*

Intercourse starts when you get up in the morning and all through the day. It is important for a husband to begin romancing his wife in the morning and later on into the night. He can accomplish this by speaking the right words to her, sending flowers, or purchasing a gift. Sometimes, it may require helping her with the dinner or helping the children with their homework, or even doing the laundry. These are non-sexual touches that women like that make them feel loved and appreciated.

It can also help relieve her of some of the tension and stress of the day.

Likewise, a woman has to begin anticipating a night of enjoyment with her husband by visualizing and using her imagination. Sex is 90% psychological and 10% physical. Since women are emotional beings, we must excite the emotions by thinking on the sexual act with our husband all throughout the day. Our thoughts dictate our actions and can determine our mood. Think about how true this is in your own life. On any given morning, a negative or positive thought will come into our mind and can set the mood for the rest of our day. This same principle applies to sexual intimacy. You can set the right mood by thinking about coming together with your spouse all through the day.

> "Romance begins when the two of you awaken to each other."

Originally, love began in a garden between a man and a woman. God created a beautiful home for Adam and Eve to enjoy intimacy with Him and each other. The Garden of Eden was a place of beauty and color. As God put the first married couple in the right environment where they could be fruitful and multiply, we must set atmosphere so that sexual intimacy can be a pleasurable experience. The environment must be perfect.

The Song of Solomon is a beautiful book that depicts the intimacy between a man and a woman, Solomon and the Shulamite woman.

Song 4:12-16 ... Dear lover and friend, you're a secret garden, a private and pure fountain. Body and soul, you are paradise, a whole orchard of succulent fruits — Ripe apricots and peaches, oranges and pears; Nut trees and cinnamon, and all scented woods; Mint and lavender, and all herbs aromatic; A garden fountain, sparkling and splashing, fed by spring waters from the Lebanon mountains. Wake up, North Wind, get moving, South Wind! Breathe on my garden, fill the air with spice fragrance. Oh, let my lover enter his garden! Yes, let him eat the fine, ripe fruits. (The Message Bible)

Ladies, your bedroom should be a physical Garden of Eden. Your bedroom speaks of intimacy; therefore it is off-limits at certain times. If you have children, your bed should not be the place where they sleep every night. This is your secret garden for you and your spouse alone, your haven of rest. Adorn it with the finest bedding you can afford. It should smell good and be clean, neat, and tidy. We need to create the right atmosphere in our home.

Make it a special place, a secret place of rendezvous for the two of you.

In this particular scripture, Solomon calls the woman *his "secret garden, his private and pure fountain"*. Not only should your bedroom be a garden, but you should be a walking Garden of Eden. Both husband and wife should smell good when you go to bed; brush your teeth, shave, take a bath, and be clean. Many times, we miss doing the practical things that can cause greater intimacy. It also shows respect for one another.

If we were to break the word intimacy down, we come up with *'In-to-me-see'*. True intimacy requires that we allow each other access into our body and soul.

1 Cor. 7:3-6...The husband should fulfill his wife's sexual needs, and the wife should fulfill her husband's needs. The wife gives authority over her body to her husband, and the husband gives authority over his body to his wife. Do not deprive each other of sexual relations, unless you both agree to refrain from sexual intimacy for a limited time so you can give yourselves more completely to prayer. Afterward, you should come together again so that Satan won't be able to tempt you because of your lack of self-control. NLT

Husbands and wives should never deprive one another sexually. This scripture shows us that to do so will allow a door for Satan to enter into the marriage. When he comes, he only has one intention, to destroy (John 10:10). The only time when a husband and wife should abstain from sexual intimacy (other than illness) is when there is a season of fasting and prayer, and even then there must be agreement between the two. When one spouse deprives the other, you open the door of temptation. Many times, the one that is being deprived begins to get involved in an extramarital affair. We know that adultery is a sin, but to withhold your body from your party is to be an accessory to the crime. We must not let Satan get an advantage, nor subject each other to fleshly temptations.

Remember only within marriage, sex is good!

- ♥ Sex is the "**WOW**" factor that keeps our eyes single.
- ♥ Sex is good physical aerobic exercise.
- ♥ Sex is a promoter of the husband's ego and a declaration of the feminine anointing of the wife.
- ♥ Sex, God's way, is for procreation, elevation, and revelation.
- ♥ As a man who loves his wife, sex is the fullness of saying to my wife, "I love you!"

EXERCISE TIME

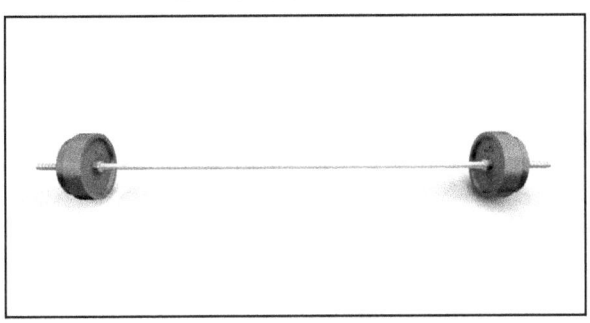

How are you tending to the garden of your marriage? Is it grown over with weeds and thorns? Do some purging and pruning.

(Take some time out together and choose to do some of these activities from the Miracle Calendar.)

DAY	ACTIVITY	SCRIPTURE
Day 1	Love Letter	Proverbs 7:3
Day 2	Spa Treatment at Home	Esther 2:12
Day 3	Beautiful Feet	Song of Solomon 7:1
Day 4	Passionate Kisses	Song of Solomon 1:2
Day 5	Evening Walk	Amos 3:3
Day 6	Soft Caress	Song of Solomon 8:3
Day 7	Tell All	Ephesians 4:15

DAY	ACTIVITY	SCRIPTURE
Day 8	*Foot Washing*	*Song of Solomon 5:3*
Day 9	*Touch & Agree*	*Matthew 18:19*
Day 10	*Laugh*	*Proverbs 17:22*
Day 11	*Time Out*	*1Peter 3:7*
Day 12	*Romantic Dinner*	*Song of Solomon 2:4*
Day 13	*Hi-Tech*	*Proverbs 22:20*
Day 14	*Food for Thought*	*Genesis 6:21*

14 Days of Love:
1. Take time out to write an intimate letter to your spouse expressing the joy and fulfillment that you find only in him. Prov. 7:3
2. Indulge your wife in the luxury of a hot, sensual bath. Play some romantic music, light candles, use oils and allow your imagination to take over. Esther 2:12
3. Buy your wife a pair of shoes, or massage her feet. Song of Sol. 7:1
4. Make sure you kiss him at least 10 times today, passionately. Song of Sol. 1:2
5. Take a stroll in the evening together and reminisce about your most memorable times together. Amos 3:3
6. Non-sexual touches (embrace; hug, talking) Song of Sol. 8:3
7. Share verbal expressions of your innermost desires (family, jobs, ministry, etc.). Eph 4:15

8. For a relaxing, soothing treat, prepare a warm, sudsy foot bath for your husband, using baby oil or lotion. Sensually massage his feet. John 13:4-5
9. Spend time praying together. Matt 18:19
10. Enjoy a time of laughter! (Comedy DVD's, movies, etc.) Tell him funny jokes; reminisce about funny experiences together. Prov. 17:22
11. Give her the day off & deal with her as the weaker vessel. Tell her that the day is hers & I'm sure she'll make the night all yours! I Pet.3:7
12. Prepare a romantic dinner for your husband and serve it to him in your bedroom.
13. Use some technology (i.e. Text, email; voicemail) to send a message of love. Prov. 22:20
14. Food for thought - go grocery shopping together. Gen. 6:21

STRENGTH TRAINING CHECK:

YOU SHOULD BE GAINING WITH EVERY TURN OF THE PAGE; MAKING SURE THAT YOU APPLY TO YOUR HEART, KNOWLEDGE SO YOUR MARRIAGE WILL BE 2 FIT 2 QUIT.

3

MY SEXUAL FITNESS, IS MY SEX LIFE IN GOOD SHAPE?

_____
_____
_____
_____
_____
_____
_____
_____
_____
_____
_____
_____
_____
_____
_____
_____
_____

POWER LIFT:
Intercourse is more than just physical. Can you remember the six types?

CHAPTER 4

FINANCIAL FITNESS: 2 MANY BILLS, 2 LITTLE MONEY

Balancing the Checkbook

Today we must see that Christian marriages are under attack. Demonic forces have taken aim at the only visible expression of Christ and His Church on earth with a vengeance. With over 50% of marriages ending in divorce, the Church is not too far behind. The devil is using three major things to destroy this holy union – communication, money, and sex.

In this chapter we will discuss money! This is an important area in a marriage, but many times, it is not considered as part of the marriage fitness plan. So many unions are destroyed because of financial matters. We must get a better understanding of the purpose, and, yes, the power of money.

Money is amoral. It has no power to make moral judgments on its own. It is directed for good or evil by the person or persons who possess it.

In marriage, money can make a spouse act and do crazy things like gamble it all away, or spend up all the money on foolish things that could have otherwise been used to pay bills. He or she may squander the savings that were designated for the children's clothes or college fund. When a couple has trouble with money, it can cause serious problems- (*like repossessions, garnishments, and foreclosures*), that can damage your creditability.

God's wisdom is greatly needed by Christian couples in money matters today like never before, because wisdom is God's supernatural "know-how" to get us on the right track in every area of our marriage! The wise man Solomon was inspired by the Holy Spirit to give us this revelation on wisdom and money in Ecclesiastes:

Eccl 7:12..." *Wisdom and money can get you almost anything, but only wisdom can save your life.*" NLT
Eccl 8:1," *There's nothing better than being wise, Knowing how to interpret the meaning of life. Wisdom puts light in the eyes, and gives gentleness to words and manners.*" (The Message Bible)

When dealing with money, we must start with what God says is first. You see, -whatever we put first in our lives determines the rest our lives.

If money is first instead of God, we are moving in the wrong direction and your money is going to be misdirected. Why? Whatever we put first deals with what we love! Usually our money problems are a love problem. You might ask, *"What's love got to do with my money?"*

Matt 6:21…"For where your treasure is, there your heart will be also." (NKJV)

Matt 6:24…"No one can serve two masters; for either he will hate the one and love the other, or else he will be loyal to the one and despise the other. You cannot serve God and mammon." (NKJV)

When God is not first in our lives, we don't have His wisdom, especially on how to handle money. Jesus said that the first thing we need to do is love the Lord!

Matt 22:37-38, "Jesus replied, 'You must love the LORD your God with all your heart, all your soul, and all your mind.' This is the first and greatest commandment." NLT

Coinciding with this commandment is the second one, "to love our neighbor as we love ourselves," which keeps us from being selfish and self-centered. Loving God and loving your neighbor becomes the foundation to handling all our money matters successfully.

Since loving God is the first principle we must apply, we need to understand why. The Bible says that love is the nature of God and the greatest demonstration of that love is giving! When God gave us His Son, He demonstrated love in the highest degree. Therefore, as Christian couples we must start with giving. God is a giver.

John 3:16... For God so loved the world, that he gave his only begotten Son, that whosoever believeth in him should not perish, but have everlasting life.

Rom 5:8...But God demonstrates His own love toward us, in that while we were still sinners, Christ died for us. NKJV

Giving has to do with honor. For example, sometimes, we may give not because the person needs it, but because we want to show them that we honor, respect, and esteem them very highly. Every Christian couple must come to an agreement that they are going to first of all give to God!

There is something very powerful about a couple who walks in agreement in the things of God. It's the power of oneness and when we are one, it releases God's commanded blessings! We have seen many marriages make a turn for the better in the area of their finances all because they came into an agreement concerning giving to God. God has given them miracle after miracle simply because they honored Him with their finances.

Just to make sure that we understand clearly what honoring God means, we are talking about the tithe and the offering.

Mal 3:8-12...Will a man rob God? Yet ye have robbed me. But ye say, Wherein have we robbed thee? In tithes and offerings. Ye are cursed with a curse: for ye have robbed me, even this whole nation. Bring ye all the tithes into the storehouse, that there may be meat in mine house, and prove me now herewith, saith the Lord of hosts, if I will not open you the windows of heaven, and pour you out a blessing, that there shall not be room enough to receive it. And I will rebuke the devourer for your sakes, and he shall not destroy the fruits of your ground; neither shall your vine cast her fruit before the time in the field, saith the Lord of hosts. And all nations shall call you blessed: for ye shall be a delightsome land, saith the Lord of hosts.

The giving of tithes and offerings releases God's blessings to our households and causes us to live in the overflow. When we tithe and give offerings He opens the windows of heaven and pours out a blessing that extends beyond our lifetime and goes to our next generation. That's an overflow!

If we want God's best for our marriage, we must begin to honor him, and sometimes this requires a sacrifice. But even when you sacrifice, you still can't beat God giving! If we want to experience overflow in our home, we must go back to honoring God with our tithes and offerings.

Lisa and I can testify personally to the faithfulness of God when you honor Him in the tithes and offering. Around 1980, we were in terrible financial shape. Our credit was shot and we barely had enough to make it. As they say, we were so broke, we couldn't pay attention. We were living in an apartment and our dream was to one day buy a house; but it looked like that would never happen. At a young age and having been married only a few years, we found ourselves in bankruptcy. This was due to loving other things and putting them ahead of God. Even though we worked hard, our pockets had holes in them! It seemed like our ends could never meet.

One day, we received the teaching on tithes and offerings. We agreed to honor God with our money and began to apply this principle in our lives. After consistently honoring God in giving, our dream of buying a house was revived and we moved into our first home 5 years later.

This is a principle every married believer should live by because this releases Gods' blessing power in your home!

**IF WE STAY WITH GOD IN PRINCIPLE,
HE WILL STAND WITH US IN POWER.**

As a couple, we must understand God's plan is that we be fruitful, which means that we would be successful, even prolific in our living in this world to show that He is good to his children! He wants you to increase, and become greater in reaching out to the lost and those in need. He wants you and yours and me and mine to do more than exist. God wants us to live in the overflow! Obeying God as a married couple in this area will not only bless you and your children's children, but it will break generational curses off your family and release generational blessings!

**THE TITHE AND OFFERING BREAK GENERATIONAL CURSES
AND RELEASES GENERATIONAL BLESSINGS.**

Prov. 13:22...A good man leaveth an inheritance to his children's children: and the wealth of the sinner is laid up for the just. NKJ

Prov. 17:6…Grandchildren are the crowning glory of the aged; parents are the pride of their children. New Living Translation

Now, let's look at some Biblical principles concerning money matters to help in getting fit financially.

SHOW ME THE MONEY

This phrase was made popular by the movie, "***Jerry McGuire***" who was a sports agent for a star athlete.

This question also needs to be asked between husbands and wives. Why? We must be accountable to each other! At the end of the day, we need to know (both the husband and wife) what has been paid and what still needs to be paid!

There is a Biblical story in the Old Testament that shows us the need to ask this question and to get an answer. It deals with a couple that were married and in ministry but never had mutual accountability in money matters.

2 Kings 4:1-7…One day the wife of a man from the guild of prophets called out to Elisha, "Your servant my husband is dead. You well know what a good man he was, devoted to GOD.

And now the man to whom he was in debt is on his way to collect by taking my two children as slaves."

"Elisha said, "I wonder how I can be of help. Tell me, what do you have in your house?" "Nothing," she said. "Well, I do have a little oil." "Here's what you do," said Elisha. "Go up and down the street and borrow jugs and bowls from all your neighbors. And not just a few — all you can get. Then come home and lock the door behind you, you and your sons. Pour oil into each container; when each is full, set it aside." She did what he said. She locked the door behind her and her sons; as they brought the containers to her, she filled them. When all the jugs and bowls were full, she said to one of her sons, "Another jug, please." He said, "That's it. There are no more jugs." Then the oil stopped. She went and told the story to the man of God. He said, "Go sell the oil and make good on your debts. Live, both you and your sons, on what's left". (The Message Bible)

In this passage of scripture we see that a prophet who served God faithfully died and left his wife and sons in debt. He left his wife with no understanding of the money matters for the home. Once she found out, to her dismay, she was broke. It seems that in this home nobody asked this question, *"Show me the money!"*

It appears the wife didn't know about the debt and in those times there was no insurance policy to fall back on. So she was caught in the middle of a money matter that she couldn't handle. You see, **before** the prophet died, she should have asked:

> *How much money do you make? Are there any debts or bills I need to know about? Do we have any savings? Is there any of your relatives that can help us get on our feet after you die?*

It is because she had no answer to any of these questions, this widow woman needed a miracle from God to keep her home and her sons from being taken as slaves!

This story is not just one that is exclusive to this widow woman, but is indicative of many Christian homes- Nobody is asking the question... **"Show me the money"**, and as a result, money, or lack of it, is bringing in undue stress, bickering, arguing, separation and the ultimate tragedy of divorce to so many marriages. So money does matter and we need to get wisdom on how to deal with the money!

There are some things that we must understand as it relates to marriage and money. It is found in the vows that we make on our wedding day. We say, "For better for worse, for richer for poorer, in sickness and in health, to love and to cherish, to have and to hold, till death do we part."

Wow! There is another part of the vow that is made when we put the ring on and it says: *"With this ring I thee wed, with my body I thee worship, and with **all my worldly goods I thee endow**: In the name of the Father, and of the Son, and of the Holy Ghost. Amen."*

Did we say that? Yes we did, and what it means is you and your spouse declared that **all** you are and **all** you have are in this marriage.

The Bible says when we make a vow to the Lord or to people, we should not defer in keeping it *(Eccl. 5:4)*. To give my all means to give the whole of me, 100% of all my earthly self, which includes my money, I give it all to my spouse. This is where the modern marriage stops. We are having a lot of money problems because we still have not understood what it means to obey the word "**all**".

There are **4 "Alls"** that we need to embrace as it relates to our money within marriage.

- ♥ <u>**ALL**</u> **the money we make in marriage belongs to God...**

Know that everything came from God and in a true sense; all of it belongs to God.

We really own nothing - we are just stewards over God's property. A steward is defined as *"one who is charged to watch over, maintain, and accept full responsibility in regards to another person's belongings or affairs."* They own nothing but have the responsibility to care for it as if they did. God is the owner; we are just caretakers. Therefore, **ALL** the money, the cars, the houses and everything we have belongs to God.

1 Chron 29:11-12... Thine, O Lord, is the greatness, and the power, and the glory, and the victory, and the majesty: ***for all that is in the heaven and in the earth is thine****; thine is the kingdom, O Lord, and thou art exalted as head above all. Both riches and honour come of thee, and* ***thou reignest over all****; and in thine hand is power and might; and in thine hand it is to make great, and* ***to give strength unto all****. KJV*

- ♥ <u>**ALL**</u> **the money that comes into the house belongs to both the husband and wife...**

Understand that ALL our money MUST leave our past single life and cleave to our present married life! We can no longer look at our finances as if we were single. The old saying rings true, *"What's yours is mine and what's mine is yours!"* Every bank account you have should have both the *husband and wife's name on them. Gen 2:22-24...And the rib, which the LORD God had taken from man, made he a woman, and brought her unto the man. And Adam said, This is now bone of my bones, and flesh of my flesh: she shall be called Woman, because she was taken out of Man. Therefore shall a man leave his father and his mother, and shall cleave unto his wife: and they shall be one flesh. KJV*

♥ **ALL you buy should be known by your spouse**

There should be "No shame in our money game!" We should not hide purchases from each other because when you hide in one area, you begin to hide in other areas until you're hiding everything from each other. We must be up front and out in the open regarding what we buy so that we maintain accountability for all funds to each other. It is called being truthful!

Gen. 2:25...And the man and his wife were both naked and were not embarrassed or ashamed in each other's presence. AMP

There are 3 things you can do to keep the peace in this area:
1. Come to an agreement on purchases above a certain amount.

Amos 3:3...Can two people walk together without agreeing on the direction? NLT

3. Establish an amount that you can spend without having to call each other. We started with $25 and as the Lord has prospered us, increased this amount.

4. Don't hold back your money from God or each other. (Josh. 7:19-26). Hiding or holding back money will trouble your household!

♥ <u>**ALL**</u> **the money in your house should be accounted for!**

We must learn to develop and stay on a budget. What is budgeting? It keeps track of our income and outgo so that our upkeep doesn't become our downfall! Here are some pointers that will aid you in budgeting.

DON'T LIVE ABOVE YOUR MEANS!!!

Never compete with another couple in possessions. Remember, you don't know where they've come from or where they've been. You must know what you can do and be satisfied and thankful at the level where God has you. There will be a day, if you continue to be consistent, that more will be added to your life. For right now, don't live above your means.

AVOID THE DEBT TRAP LIKE THE PLAGUE

Prov. 22:26-27…Don't agree to guarantee another person's debt or put up security for someone else. If you can't pay it, even your bed will be snatched from under you. NLT

Rom. 13:8…Don't run up debts, except for the huge debt of love you owe each other. When you love others, you complete what the law has been after all along. MSG

Debt is a trap that has had many bound up. William V. Thompson, author of "**Debt Trap**" says, "It enslaves people to its will and hinders them from following God's plan for their lives. **It is the visible manifestation of an invisible devil.**" It functions in the same capacity as the devil, who comes to steal, kill, and destroy (John 10:10).

Financial problems are the number one reason for divorce, and family destruction. Many couples spend countless hours arguing over money. Children suffer because one or more of the parents are out of the home, leaving them left to themselves.

It is imperative, that if we are to fulfill the will of God on earth, in our marriages and advance His Kingdom, the Church must address the issue of debt.

The Great Commission suffers because of this problem. Not only are individuals bound up in debt, but also the Church.

The Word of God is replete with instructions on being debt-free, and we must get a vision for our marriage and family of becoming debt-free. It is not an enemy that cannot be conquered. We can slay this giant, if we follow the principles of the Word of God, and the discipline of the Holy Spirit.

15 STEPS TO FINANCIAL FREEDOM

1. Recognize God as owner and provider of all basic goods in life. Lev. 25:23; 1 Chron. 29:10-12; Ps 24:1; Ps. 50:10; Hag. 2:8
2. Honor God by being a faithful tithe-paying member of your local church. – Mal. 3:8-10; Prov. 3:9
3. Give to others – Luke 6:38; Eccl. 11:1-2; Matt. 6:1-4; Rom. 12:12:13
4. Have a good consistent work ethic. - 1 Thess. 4:11; 2 Thess. 3:10,12
5. Deal with the root of the problem, why you got into debt in the first place (i.e. covetousness, which leads to greed and overindulgence; envy or trying to **"keep up with the Jones's"** – Heb. 13:5

6. **MINIMUM PAYMENT IS THE DEVIL** – Always pay more than the minimum payment. If at all possible, pay the minimum payment plus the finance charge. When you pay only the minimum payment, the majority of your payment goes toward the interest and not the outstanding balance. Credit card companies earn about 75% of their revenues from people who don't pay in full each month.

7. If you must use a credit card, try to only purchase amounts that you will be able to pay the balance in full within 30 days.

8. Write down all of your debts, listing the balance owed, minimum payment due, and interest rate of each. (You must get a vision, a picture of your debt, and a prophetic revelation of how you will conquer it. Hab. 2:2)

- Begin to pay off the debt with the lowest balance 1st.

- After paying off one bill, take the amount you were paying on that one, and apply that amount to the bill with the next lowest balance. Keep doing this until all are paid. Many credit card debts can be paid off within 2 years (except mortgage and car payments).

9. Get on a budget and stick to it. Control your spending with the help of the Holy Spirit.

10. Be an accountable to someone. If need be, find a good Christian Financial Counselor.

11. **Save! Save! Save!** – 1 Tim. 6:19. We must learn to lay up in store a good foundation against the times to come (times of lack, famine, or emergency.) Discipline yourself to save something every paycheck, if no more than $10-20 a week.

12. If you are renting, take immediate steps to purchase a home. A home is an investment, an appreciating item, unlike a new car, which depreciates as soon as You drive it off the lot. The true wealth is what you own.

13. Make cash purchases, and beware of 90 day same as cash purchases. If you don't pay the outstanding balance within that time frame, interest is tacked on from the day of the purchase.

14. Don't co-sign for anyone! – Prov. 6:1-5

15. Sow into someone else's life. Help someone else get out of debt. When you sow your seed into another's life, it creates a harvest in yours. Gal. 6:7

4

MY FINANCIAL FITNESS, IS MY MONEY IN GOOD SHAPE?

_____
_____
_____
_____
_____
_____
_____
_____
_____
_____
_____
_____
_____
_____
_____
_____
_____

POWER LIFT:
15 Steps to Financial Freedom is a good guide. What steps do you need to take to become financially free?

CHAPTER 5

PHYSICAL FITNESS: 2 FAT, 2 SKINNY

How to Be Physically Fit For the Life of Your Marriage

1 Cor. 6:19-20...What? Know ye not that your body is the temple of the Holy Ghost which is in you, which ye have of God, and ye are not your own? For ye are bought with a price: therefore glorify God in your body, and in your spirit, which are God's. KJV

The last area we need to focus on if we are to be fitly joined together in marriage is being physically fit. We must have balance in our lives. The Bible states, *"A false balance is an abomination unto the Lord, but a just weight is his delight."* (Prov. 11:1) As stated before, we are a tri-partite being. We are a spirit, we possess a soul, and we live in a body. All of these areas are affected by each other. Jesus said, *"...the spirit is indeed willing, but the flesh is weak."* (Matt. 26:41) Our spirit and soul can be limited by the weaknesses that are in our body. Many times, sexual intimacy cannot be realized because of ailments in our body;

therefore, we must address this issue. If we don't understand the purpose of a thing, abuse is inevitable. We must honor God in every area of our life. Our bodies belong to God and taking care of our physical body is one way this is accomplished.

1 Cor. 10:31...Whether therefore ye eat, or drink, or whatsoever ye do, do all to the glory of God. KJV

We should eat to live, not live to eat. Many of us are the worst of violators in this area. It's food that plunged the human race into sin. Food is not what is harming us, but how much of it we are consuming, and the way the food is presented to us.

Gen 1:29-31...And God said, See, I have given you every plant yielding seed that is on the face of all the land and every tree with seed in its fruit; you shall have them for food. And to all the animals on the earth and to every bird of the air and to everything that creeps on the ground — to everything in which there is the breath of life — I have given every green plant for food. And it was so. And God saw everything that He had made, and behold, it was very good (suitable, pleasant) and He approved it completely. (AMP)

Gen 2:9...And out of the ground the Lord God made to grow every tree that is pleasant to the sight or to be desired — good (suitable, pleasant) for food. (AMP)

We must be careful of the lust of the eyes, even in our appetite for food. Some foods are loaded with sugars and harmful preservatives. Too much of anything is not good.

Prov. 23:1-3...While dining with a ruler, pay attention to what is put before you. If you are a big eater, put a knife to your throat; don't desire all the delicacies, for he might be trying to trick you. NLT

This takes discipline and self-control, which is a fruit of the Spirit. We are called to a disciplined life in every area. We must sanctify our bodies, set them apart for God's holy use. Our bodies are to be holy vessels unto the Lord *(Rom. 12:1-2).* Our body needs to come under the control of the Holy Spirit.

Not only do our bodies belong to God, but they belong to our spouse as well.

1 Cor 7:4...The wife gives authority over her body to her husband, and the husband gives authority over his body to his wife. (New Living Translation)

It is vitally important that we keep our bodies in good physical shape for our mates to enjoy. We understand that we live in a fallen world, and there are so many sicknesses and diseases in the world. Many of them are a direct result of the increase of sin; even the ground is rebelling.

Yet, there are things that we are doing that violate the dietary laws that produce unnecessary illness and hardships on our spouse and family.

All diseases are not hereditary. Many sicknesses are inherited only because of generational *diets*. We pass down harmful recipes from one generation to the next. "Big Mama always fixed greens with fatback and so that's the way I fix mine." But too much fatback is unhealthy, and can result in high blood pressure, heart disease, diabetes, etc. And we pass these same habits on to our husbands and our children by feeding them foods that are unhealthy.

I am a firm believer in living a healthy lifestyle. Having been a victim of yo-yo dieting for so long, I have discovered that dieting does not work. There is no magic formula to losing weight and keeping it off. Oops! I know that is not encouraging, but it is the truth. Diet alone never works!

Have you ever asked yourself, "Why is there such an obsession with losing weight, especially with women?" It seems the more obsessed I get with it, the fatter I become. As Paul said in **Romans 7:24, "I've tried everything and nothing helps. I'm at the end of my rope. Is there no one who can do anything for me? (Message Bible).** Let me say that

I understand that in this particular verse Paul was speaking about sin that lies within our members. But isn't that the real issue? Was it not food that started this whole sin cycle anyway?

Gen 2:15-17...Then the Lord God took the man and put him in the Garden of Eden to tend and keep it. And the Lord God commanded the man, saying, "Of every tree of the garden you may freely eat; but of the tree of the knowledge of good and evil you shall not eat, for in the day that you eat of it you shall surely die."

Gen 3:1-7...Now the serpent was more cunning than any beast of the field which the Lord God had made. And he said to <u>the woman,</u> "Has God indeed said, 'You shall not eat of every tree of the garden'?" And <u>the woman</u> said to the serpent, "We may eat the fruit of the trees of the garden; but of the fruit of the tree which is in the midst of the garden, God has said, 'You shall not eat it, nor shall you touch it, lest you die.'" Then the serpent said to the woman, "You will not surely die. For God knows that in the day you eat of it your eyes will be opened, and you will be like God, knowing good and evil." So when <u>the woman</u> saw that the tree was good for food, that it was pleasant to the eyes, and a tree desirable to make one wise, she took of its fruit and ate. <u>She also gave to her husband with her, and he ate.</u> NKJ

We can see that our first parents got into trouble because of their choice of food. Thank God for His redemptive plan, but look at the consequences we sometimes have to pay for our sins. It brought calamity, not only to their spiritual lives, but their natural lives because it shortened their days.

Today this is still an issue, especially with the female gender. We can see that Satan targeted the woman. Could this possibly be one of the reasons we are so obsessed with weight? But you may ask, "Didn't Christ redeem us from the fall? Then why are we still plagued with obesity and all kinds of sickness?" It goes back to **choices and obedience.**

The Way To A Man's Heart Is Through His Belly

Presentation is everything. We like to eat food that is appealing to the eye and the appetite. God planted the various trees in the Garden for Adam and Eve and made it presentable. Likewise, the devil presented a fruit to Eve in an appealing way. It is said that the way to a man's heart is through his belly. This is not written in the scripture, but if I can use my sanctified imagination, I believe that Eve took an apple and made an apple pie and served it to Adam!
Food is not evil in itself, just like money is not evil. It's the love of food and money. The devil

is always trying to pervert what God calls good. He tried to tempt Jesus the same way. He uses the same old cheese to trap us.

Matt 4:1-4...Then Jesus was led by the Spirit into the wilderness to be tempted there by the devil. For forty days and forty nights he fasted and became very hungry. During that time the devil came and said to him, "If you are the Son of God, tell these stones to become loaves of bread." But Jesus told him, "No! The Scriptures say, 'People do not live by bread alone, but by every word that comes from the mouth of God.'" NLT

Many of the diseases we suffer with today can be **cured** with proper dietary behavior. I believe our Creator has given us everything we need that pertains to life and godliness *(2 Peter 1:3)*. All we need to do is apply the principles of the Word of God. I have discovered a simple way of losing weight and keeping it off, but more importantly of staying healthy. I must say that I have not gained complete victory, but I do know that it works. I call it **THE D.E.W.** – a system of **D**iet, **E**xercise, and **W**ater.

Diet

We live in a fallen world whereby even our food supply has been corrupted and contaminated. Many of the vitamins and nutrients have been stripped from our foods by over processing and preservatives. Sugar and salt consumption is at an all time high, not only in our food, but much of what we drink. If you would do your research, you will find that a meal in many of our fast food restaurants is well over the daily requirements (2000 calories per day), and even our dine-in restaurants serve food portions that are double the requirements.

The first thing we must do is start eating healthy and stop eating empty calories (sugary and starchy foods). A calorie is defined as a unit of energy supplied by the food we consume. It is a measure of energy or fuel for your body. *A calorie is a calorie regardless of its source.* All foods contain calories.

However, in order for your body to run properly, it must have a balance of calories and a proper nutrition of food. The body needs:

1. **Protein** (found in meat, poultry, fish, eggs, and dairy products, nuts, grains and beans) to help build and maintain muscle.

2. **Fat** – Yes! Fat doesn't make you fat. Eating too much fat (or any other food) makes you fat. It's essential for good skin, helps your digestive system, and is like a coat for your body to keep you from freezing to death.

3. **Carbohydrates**. Get it out of your mind that carbohydrates are bad! Like fat, too much of anything is not good (except the things of God). Carbohydrates are our body's primary source of fuel or energy. However, it includes sugars and starches, which when consumed in large quantities is harmful; therefore, we must limit our in take on these.

*Prov. 25:16...Do you like honey **(SWEETS)**? Don't eat too much, or it will make you sick! NLT*

Prov. 25:16...When you're given a box of candy, don't gulp it all down; eat too much chocolate and you'll make yourself sick; (THE MESSAGE BIBLE)

4. As much as possible, build your meals around fruits, vegetables, and whole grains, which are the good carbohydrates.

5. **Fiber**. Fiber is absolutely necessary for good health. God has designed everything to have a process of elimination. Fiber does that because it softens and adds bulk to your stools. It has many more benefits. We should eat at least 20-35 grams of fiber every day which can be found in oats, nuts, fruits and most vegetables, brown rice, beans.

When trying to lose weight, we must remember that one pound of body weight is equal to 3,500 calories. Depending on what your goal is, you need to regulate your caloric intake. Here are a few quick notes:

1. To **maintain** your weight, eat and burn the same number of calories.
2. To **decrease** your weight, burn more calories than you eat.
3. To **increase** your weight, eat more calories than you burn (I wish I could be so blessed!).
4. Eat **smaller** portions.
5. Eat **3 meals** a day (to include a protein, vegetable, and a carbohydrate).
6. Eat **2 snacks** a day (this may include a vegetable/fruit along with a small portion size of protein).
7. Eat at least **every 3-4 hours**. Your body will burn the food quicker. One of the mistakes we make is to eat 1-2 heavy meals a day. By doing this, you confuse your body. A reverse reaction takes place and your body begins to hold onto the fat because it thinks you're starving it.

There are a number of good weight programs available today to help with your weight loss goals. However, it doesn't matter which one you choose, none of them will work if you don't have a mind to stick to it, and to discipline yourself.

is better to reset your thinking concerning losing weight. Stop dieting and change your eating life style. Make a choice to eat right for the rest of your life.

Exercise:

If you want to move fat, then you must move your body. There is no substitute for exercise. The only way to **maintain** a healthy weight is exercise. God did not make us to be sedentary. In Genesis 2, we see that He put man in the Garden and told him to dress it and keep it, which required physical labor. The same applies today. Our Creator is wise.

We become fat when we sit at a computer all day long and then get on the elevator (instead of using the stairs) and walk a few steps to our car that has been parked as close to the front door as possible, only to stop at the drive-thru restaurant and get a fast meal to go home and pick up our remote to watch our favorite television program that is loaded with fattening food commercials that seduce us to snack on until we go to bed, only to rise up the next morning to drink our caffeinated coffee and sugary donuts. No wonder America is so fat!

We need to get in at least three hours of exercise per week or 30 minutes of cardio exercise per day. The body needs to get moving. The best time for us is in the morning. Exercise burns energy (fat) and also gives you energy.

On a personal note, both of us have begun a rigorous exercise regimen. Keith has a personal trainer who is a local pastor with a passion to take care of God's temple. His motto on exercise is to never stop, to make it a lifetime matter. So when I go to the gym, I'm there to train my body to love exercise, not just to work out! You can work the total body by doing cardio, floor exercises, abdominal crunches, and weight training. Lisa also goes to the gym, but most of the time keeps up a good regiment with the use of DVD's and home exercise equipment.

Exercise is vitally important in these last days because a prepared body is needed to carry a prepared message.

We live such sedentary lives which makes the body susceptible to all kinds of diseases. A lot of stress can also be relieved through exercise.

The body is meant for motion. So rise up and put your body in motion! You'll feel better and look better for your spouse. Both of you can have a body that is 2 Fit 2 Quit.

Water:

Water is essential. You can live without food longer than you can go without water. When our Lord fasted 40 days and nights, it is implied in Matt. 4:2 that he fasted from food only, not water.

"And when he had fasted forty days and forty nights, he was afterward an hungered."

We are fearfully and wonderfully made. Our body is 66% water; therefore we need to stay hydrated. Drinking the right amount of water keeps the kidneys flowing and the skin glowing, and gives you a sense of fullness. We should drink ½ of our body weight of water. For instance, if you weigh 150 lbs., you should drink at least 75 oz. of water per day. I have found if I drink at least 10 oz. of water before eating a meal, I am less likely to overeat because I have a sense of fullness.

In conclusion, we need to make a genuine commitment to take care of this temple of the Holy Ghost. Jesus came to give us life – abundant life. God wants not only to give us healing, but health.

Taking care of our body is part of the abundant life. We have a work to do in these last days and we need to be healthy and strong. We need to be *fit to fight, so we can have a good life* for the sake of our family and loved ones.

5

PHYSICAL FITNESS, AM I IN GOOD PHYSICAL SHAPE?

_____
_____
_____
_____
_____
_____
_____
_____
_____
_____
_____
_____
_____
_____
_____

POWER LIFT:
Physical fitness will require more "Fruit of the Spirit". Can you stand to increase your fruit (discipline and self-control) intake?

CHAPTER 6
FIT FOR ETERNITY

I believe that God has saved the best for last. We are the "end-time harvest" that will see the manifestation of Jesus and His Bride, the Church. We must get filled with the Spirit of God and allow Him to fill our cups – our lives and our marriages – so the world can see that God is truly among His people.

We celebrate marriage on earth. But there is coming a day when we all will be part of an Eternal Marriage – the Marriage Supper of the Lamb and we will be the Bride of Christ. This is just a rehearsal. We shall reign with Christ on the throne.

Rev 19:7-9...let us be glad and rejoice, and give honour to him: for the marriage of the lamb is come, and his wife hath made herself ready. and to her was granted that she should be arrayed in fine linen, clean and white: for the fine linen is the righteousness of saints. and he saith unto me, write, blessed are they which are called unto the marriage supper of the lamb. And he saith unto me, these are the true sayings of God. (KJV)

Prophetically speaking, we are approaching the third day, which speaks of resurrection. Jesus was raised **bodily** on the third day, and God will raise up our bodies on the third day.

Now may the God of peace Himself sanctify you completely; and may your whole spirit, soul, and body be preserved blameless at the coming of our Lord Jesus Christ (1 Thess. 5:23-24 NKJV)

EXERCISE TIME

If you have not done so, the first step you need to take in order to be fit for eternity is to receive the message of salvation. You must be born again. You can do so by trusting Jesus Christ to be your Lord and Savior. All it takes is for you to be sincere before God and follow these prayer steps. Ask Jesus Christ to come into your heart.

1. Admit that you are a sinner. Rom. 3:23 says, "All have sinned and come short of the glory of God."

2. Believe that Jesus paid the penalty for your sins and through faith in His blood, you can be forgiven and receive eternal life. Ponder these scriptures:

    Rom. 6:23: "For the wages of sin is death, but the gift of God is eternal life through Jesus Christ our Lord.

    John 3:16: "For God so loved the world that He gave His only begotten Son, that whosoever believes in Him should not perish, but have eternal life.

3. Confess your sins and ask Jesus Christ to forgive you. 1 John 1:9..."If we confess our sins, he is faithful and just to forgive us our sins, and to cleanse us from all unrighteousness.

    Rom. 10:9-10: "...that if you confess with your mouth the Lord Jesus and believe in your heart that God has raised Him from the dead, you will be saved. For with the heart one believes unto righteousness, and with the mouth confession is made unto salvation.

Pray from your heart and mean it.

"Lord Jesus. I need you. I admit that I have gone astray from you and messed up my life. I am a sinner. Please forgive me of my sins. I ask you to come into my heart and be my Lord and Savior. Live your life in me and live your life through me. I give you my heart. Thank you Jesus for dying on the cross for me. Thank you for saving me. Amen!

If you've done this, God promises that you are saved.

Ephesians 2:8-9..."For by grace you have been saved through faith, and that not of yourselves; *it is* the gift of God, not of works, lest anyone should boast.

You are now a new creation with a new life. 2 Corinthians 5:17-18..."Therefore, if anyone *is* in Christ, *he is* a new creation; old things have passed away; behold, all things have become new."

Through Jesus Christ, you have been made right with God and you can now live a new life. He will live it through you. All you have to do is walk in obedience to Him. Make sure you go to a good Holy Ghost filled, Bible-believing church where you can continue to grow in this new life. As you do, you too will be 2 Fit 2 Quit for ETERNITY!

6

ETERNAL FITNESS, AM I FIT FOR ETERNITY?

_____
_____
_____
_____
_____
_____
_____
_____
_____
_____
_____
_____
_____
_____
_____
_____
_____
_____

POWER LIFT:
Have you accepted God's gift of salvation to secure your place in eternity, with Christ?

REFERENCES

Scripture references from various Biblical Translations included in this book.

Special thanks to:
Zondervan and Biblica for use of the KJV and NIV.

Thomas Nelson Publishers for the use of *New King James Version* of the Holy Bible.

Tyndale House Publishers for permission to use the *New Living Translation*.

Navpress Publishers for permission to use *The Message Translation*.

Excerpt from *Debt Trap by William V. Thompson and Fatin Horton*. Copyright ©1999. Reprinted with permission of William V. Thompson.

Article entitled, New Marriage and Divorce Statistics Released, Reprinted with permission from Barna Group. ©March 31, 2008.

Reference made to movie: Uptown Saturday Night. Dir. Sidney Poitier. Perfs. Bill Cosby, Sidney Portier. Film. Warner Bros, 1974.

Reference made to movie: The Color Purple.
Dir: Steven Spielberg. Perfs. Whoopie Goldberg, Danny Glover. Film. Warner Bros, 1985

Quote from Apostle Halton "Skip" Horton.
DayStar Tabernacle International, Douglasville, GA.

Humor Quote from Apostle Louis Greenup.
Christ the Deliverer Assembly, Greenwell Springs, LA.

Special thanks to the cartoonists for their willingness to share their talents with us:

Mike Waters
Email: mike@joyfultoons.com
Web: www.joyfultoons.com

Randy Glasbergen, Cartoonist
E-mail: randy@glasbergen.com
Web: www.glasbergen.com

Zahn Carroll
Web: www.cartoonstock.com

Marital Fitness...2 FIT 2 QUIT

www.ingramcontent.com/pod-product-compliance
Lightning Source LLC
Chambersburg PA
CBHW051452290426
44109CB00016B/1723